QUICK

Peter Spafford was born in 1956, and lived in London, Manchester and Hull before settling in his current home, Leeds. His plays (musical and otherwise) have been performed throughout the country, and have occasionally graced the airwaves of Radio 4. He is a founder member of the band Schwa, is currently Director of Spoken Word at Chapel FM, and does a variety of writing work in prisons, schools, museums, and hospitals. He was longlisted in the 2015 National Poetry Competition. *Quick* is his first collection.

Quick

PETER SPAFFORD

Valley Press

First published in 2016 by Valley Press
Woodend, The Crescent, Scarborough, YO11 2PW
www.valleypressuk.com

ISBN 978-1-908853-66-0
Cat. no. VP0083

www.valleypressuk.com/authors/peterspafford

Supported using public funding by
ARTS COUNCIL
ENGLAND
LOTTERY FUNDED

Contents

Acknowledgements

My mother knew much poetry by heart and spoke it to me as a small child. I can still hear it.

My father was a skilled medical practitioner. He was also an unpublished poet.

R. G. Gregory set me on the road and gave me the shove I needed.

Nigel Pollitt has always been a warm updraught beneath my writing, and a disciplined exemplar.

Barney Bardsley is a fellow-climber on the writing wall. We wave to each other often.

Catherine Staples, Meg Peacocke, and Stephen Clark helped invaluably with the refining of these poems.

Jamie McGarry at Valley Press has kept faith with me. Rosa Campbell has been quietly helpful.

I am more grateful to Mary Cooper as a precise critic and loving friend than I can possibly say.

For Laurie and Owen

Andante

Transitional

'The life of a man is the swift flight of a sparrow through
the banqueting hall'
THE VENERABLE BEDE

First, that crazed tattoo on the buffed floor,
woman screaming, ramming a stack of trays,
basket a still-life spilt, of apples bouncing, tins a-skitter.
Then himself, rearing, boxing the air.

Who will tell from whence he bolted:
Light Brigade, Edwardian funeral, Gloucester Hunt?
Catch that whinny, watch him skate and skirl
up the fruits, down the salads aisle.

Barrows of kumquats, apricots, tumble, like tables in a temple.
Eyes white-frightful, knowing himself displaced from myth,
he turns now, flings his mane once more,
as towers of herbs, cities of spices, fall.

Take stock, before you sweep the scattered basmati and re-stack
    the beans.
Before that furtive glance at the phone, before the next poem,
hold him, fuming, in your eye; not as augury or metaphor,
just and for all he was, a horse in Tesco.

Posed, 1956

I'm a porker, I'm a snorker,
a mound of flesh, a smudge, a piece of white fudge
plumped on the bed, blessings on my avocado pear head,
sat straight up, a giant mother hand from the edge of the
    photo propping my back up,
grinner, double-chinner, the original sinner, baldy Yul Brynner,
I'm a fat pud, a clean soap sud, I'm here, I'm god.

Museum of Writing

Triangular stylus, lead stylus.
Goose quill, swan quill, mapping pens, brush pens.
Pencils: carbon, charcoal. Erasers. What you would expect.
But in this museum:

Goethe's blotter, Kafka's bed,
the matches Max Brod almost used to light the diaries.
Beckett's flask, a pink serviette from the Edinburgh caff
where Joanne Rowling stared at a pad of lined A4.

On velvet plush a packet of featherlite
bought in The Globe on Bedale Street by 'Bridget Jones'.
A phial of brownish water from the Ouse
drained from the lungs of Virginia Woolf.

Put on the headphones, hear for yourself the rat-scrat of quill
and the farts of Montaigne, the sigh of Proust
in the cork lined room, the breath of Heloise
on the neck of Abelard.

In the atrium here, the wince of chalk on blackboard,
the smell of Quink; an ache in the arm shaken out by a scribe
on an autumn night in 1082. And down in the basement,
the rattle of the ink jet printer as it jams
and jams and jams on page 94.

The pebble my mother used as a paperweight next
to a poem the young lad Carlton wrote in his Doncaster nick.
In a jar at the back, the pickled eyes of a man who watched
the library of Alexandria burn.

And here in the hall under buffed glass, a shopping list found
in the handbag of Sarah Bardsley, deceased,
near an empty drawer containing the story of her long, full life
that no one wrote down.

Swimming in Nidderdale

For Stas

Love this language. Do, love it.
Take *Nidd*. River Nidd, liquid, solid,
beneath that stained-green glass
the summer beech leaves
make of light.

River Nidd, dribbling beneath its crone skin
boulders stitched with brachiopods.
Stout. Guinness, here in the shadow.
Nidd meant *shining*
in older English.

All rivers shine in the eyes of one who loves this water,
knows this place, vale of the Nidd.
And so we learn, before the Viking farmer came,
Romans mined their lead up on that hill.
Nitidus. Latin for shining (not in the school book).
Nitid. Nidd.

Love this language. Do, love it. Roman, far from home,
pronounces the river his, his word.
Tongues, like currents in mineral waters,
roll and rock the word around.
Seasons, kings, centuries, pass.
And so the word, smoothed by usage like a stone,
is *Nidd*, is mine.

Better Late

For R and R on their wedding, after
meeting twenty-five years before.

The young man throws a Frisbee,
flings it away, like a chance,
a rare opportunity.

It soars over the sea,
then hangs a moment, a year,
a quarter of a century

Returning to him now,
angling down through the years.
The older man catches it cleanly.

Field of Glass

For several weeks in the summer of 2011, games on club cricket grounds
in West Yorkshire were endangered by an unusual form of vandalism.
Fragments of glass were found sprinkled over the outfield.

Do you ponder why
I walk this field
at night?

I was born on pavilion steps,
beneath a field of darkness
set with stars,

laid, in practice cradle,
a slip of a catch,
in the wood.

Before my good eye focused,
form was red
on green.

My growing measured
against a stump, I learnt to count
in sixes and fours.

His fingers shone
with linseed oil. He smelt
of leather

and dark male piss
on sun-hot
iron:

God, the groundsman,
weather-tuned, tender
with grass,

marker of boundaries,
heavy roller, Father
Time.

The words he gave me
were hard and round
in my mouth.

I dreamt of girls,
but woke, snagged in a tumble
of nets,

(next man in, but Did Not Bat
on that sweet
strip).

Only a game, they
told me, a
game.

And you wonder
why I pace this field
at night,

why, beneath crushed stars,
I scatter this
seed?

Mary, 1993

First sight? Bird, sharp;
eyes restless, tiny hands;
      a chirp of flight, alert
to stay, observe, yet
      anxious to be gone on some
bird business of her own.

Love? Not sure. Thrilled a little
to have kept her
      still for a second, ruffled
the organised feathers, unsurprised
      if never to catch that
twitcher's glimpse again.

Memories of Hohenschönhausen, East Germany

Hohenschönhausen was a Stasi detention centre in the former GDR
where political prisoners were held.

Piece of piss. You don't need much.
Think everyday objects. Kitchen. Greenhouse.

We used a bucket. Steel, with a rim on the base. Getting the
    picture? See where I'm going
with this? Wires and sockets, they're for the flicks.
It's a piece of piss,

You think. To kneel on a bucket. Five minutes. Ten. Blind-
    fold. Knees on the rim, your weight
bearing down, for hours. Fall off. Back on the bucket. Fall off.
Back on the bucket.

Simple, you think. An upturned pail. Could have thought of
    that yourself, you think.
And that's my point. Don't need to be clever. Common sense.
And whatever's to hand.

Mistypes 1

Sandwishes

Dune sand wishes to be
splashed, spumed at ocean lip,
churned by storm-brewed breakers.

Soaked sand wishes to be up by the cliff grass,
dry and white, warm
for toes to wiggle in.

Most sand wishes to be
in your bed, in a fold of sheet,
chafing sun-raw skin,

or clashed between
unsuspecting teeth
in a chicken salad roll.

Some sand wishes to be artfully layered
with different-coloured sand
in a long glass cup,

envies shells their hollowed caves
where sea roars
in the ears of children.

All sand wishes to be separate,
each grain weighed, examined minutely, uniquely sided,
gifted like diamonds.

Sand remembers rock and boulder,
before rain's pecking, wind's wearing,
ground it down.

Something I Made

For Sue

The making I like.
Handbuilding, wedging, turning.
But no, not the finish, other people seeing,
the glazing. For that,
you have to be neat.

We walk between.
I live here, you live there.
In the space between we walk
for the colours, the smells of walking,
or just to keep warm.

If I made you a gift,
you would see something
I had not intended.

That earthenware pot. I'd feathered too deep
and the clay showed through.
But that imperfection
was what you liked.

What would I make you?
A stoneware mug,
but I do earthenware.
Earthenware chips.

If I did mugs, I would make you one
big and white, well-finished,
with specks showing through
from the clay-body. Subtle.
If I did subtle.

We walk between.
The making I like.
But no, not the finish, and you seeing.
You might find something
I had not intended.

Divided

I have a sister, a twin. We were both
put out for adoption but given
to different families. We have never
met, and that's a strange thing.
I am seen all over. Lincoln, Sleaford,
places I have never been. And

Strangers are always approaching me,
in shops, on pavements, in cinemas,
tapping on my shoulder. 'Hello!' then
'Sorry, I thought…' We're bound to meet.
One day, walking towards each other down the street
she will stop, I will stop, or I won't.

Adagio

People With Kids

People with kids look tired.
People with kids age fast and put on weight rapidly.
People with kids are always busy but get nothing done

and drive to places that kids like
so the kids have other kids to be with and the people with kids
have other people to leave their kids with
when they want to feel like people without kids.

People with kids are grown-up people.
People with kids sigh and smile and say
kids change your life, you can`t imagine.

People with kids say sorry for talking about the kids
but talk about their kids.

People with kids call kids small people.

People with kids have one way of talking to people with kids
and another way of talking to people without kids.

People with kids sit and talk to each other about how
having kids makes them remember all sorts of stuff about
when they were kids and how their parents talked to them as kids
but now they hear themselves saying the same things
to their own kids, isn`t it amazing?

People with kids pity people without kids.

People with kids are delighted when the people without kids
announce they are going to have kids
because now they will no longer have to
envy the people without kids all the things they can do
and the holidays they can have without kids because
now those people will start feeling just as
old and fucked as they do, which serves them right
for not having kids before.

People with kids have more kids.

Inconceivable

This time last year at Bossall
we saw the violet and primrose under the yew
and felt our chance missed.

Perhaps to salvage the lost spring,
we bought at Buttercrambe
a cluster of roots for the garden
to cancel with bold strikes of renewal
this small death.

We did not know, how could we know,
that already he was moored, a raft of cells
with two days purchase on the slippery
face of life.

Today at Bossall under the yew
we looked for the moist cool flames again.
And look, here in our garden, like a kept promise,
the snowdrops we carried from Buttercrambe
and planted in hope, or in memory, then.

After Birth

It was a slab of slither,
a glossy wobble tinged with green
attached to a see-through bathing cap.

It was a stopped Dalí clock on a sheet,
a dark jelly freed from a secret mould.
It was a tree of veins in a leaf of meat.

Take it, we'd only burn it, she said.

It was a chemical threat trussed with tape.
It was pass-the-parcel in a swaddle of placky bag.
It was takeaway scandal, McDonald's for Hannibal Lecter or
   the dog.

Some people bury them and plant a tree, she said.

So we took it home to the deep freeze
where it stayed all Christmas and New Year till
we chipped it out, needing the space for peas.

It was a brick of brown jam.
It was a cold gem in a twist of granite.
It was a solid rock of misjudgement.

In a winter's light with a ringing spade
I hacked a hole, stowed it briskly in the freezer of the earth,
embarrassed to consider what now I buried
with such glib unceremony:
house of origin, kernel of his birth.

Having no faith or tree to plant,
I placed a gnome to mark the place.
Months later, toppling the ironic obelisk,
I dug the patch beneath to air for spring.

It was a lick of wet rust in the clay.
It was a miracle all over again.
It was good soil for the garden.

Found Object

The child has lost a toy: knight with plume,
cowboy with white sombrero,
Cherokee Brave.

Looks in the fort, the garage, the train set.
Lorries, arrows. Lifts the lid
of the long green box

And there it floats, bottle of scotch,
conspicuous only because not right,
adrift amongst cars and daleks.

'Look,' he says. His mother turns,
the sight of it draining
the smile from her face.

'Your father,' she says, begins to say.
And the fine vapour of truth
is unstoppered, away.

Player

I find them in the attic,
photos rimed with dust; black and white.
Teams of boys, men in colours.
Rugby. Cricket.

There he is, standing tall, centre row.
And now I have begun.
Entranced with the scrunch of glass,
I smash each one.

Why? my mother asks, puzzled.
Dad says nothing. Never one for slipper or belt.
But now I have boys of my own
I can guess how he felt.

Baby Machine

A sound, a colour,
and the neck swivels,
unstable, mechanical,
the body a fleshy motor of desire
from which an arm springs,
fronds of fingers feathering the air, the hand
an anemone-mouth of appetite
for which all casual passing life is meat.
The baby is a baby is a baby.

Love Talk

This is a new species of desire,
your weight on the bench of my arm,
the smell of your nape,
I crave them like a lover,
play over in stale absence
the bright mint of your smile,
its balm of recognition,

Hoard your gestures,
take them out walking or into the meeting,
finger their fugitive shapes,
smile at the air. Like you,
I'm fresh-invented, newly made,
a father gaping at the child,
knowing who created who.

The Crying Baby

The baby was crying.

The baby was crying,
scratching his hoarse graffiti
on the clean space of the night
and his father wanted him to stop.

The books said rock him so he did.
The leaflets said hold him so he did.

He tried it all. He even tried slamming
the door of his heart shut and leaving the room
but the food he ate in the kitchen tasted of the hard bursting
sound of baby and the crying prised the door ajar.

He tried walking with the baby.
He tried driving the baby in the car.
He drove till the petrol gauge blinked
and still the baby cried, a scrawny power
jerked up bitter from the gut of the world.

He filled the car and drove to the sea,
(faced with that other unstoppable power
the baby must surely stop)
but the baby went on crying,
the baby went on crying,
the baby went on.

He took the baby to the rocks.
The waves were white dissolving snarls in the darkness
and still the baby cried.

He took the baby to the black water and lowered him.
Now the baby would sense sea and see sense and
cease.

But by the time the salt darkness should have licked
the screams and the baby away,
the tide had gone out,
there was no water.

At dawn he carried the baby to the top of the cliffs.
The seagulls giddied below him,
his belly lurched to fly,
but by the time he had let the baby like a feather into the air
(the father's body filling with a vast remembered
peace the size of space) a draught of wind had plucked
the baby up and floated him, landed him
back in his basket at home where the father found him
asleep.

Return

The last time I saw my father we were smarting from a row.
A classic departure: an open return, and the long local train
    gathering pace;
I can flash it up now,
him standing there, the pouches of sadness in his face
and the last chance bleeding.

When I walk back from the train I am swinging a summerful
    of light
on a thumb that has hitched through Italy and France from a
    Mediterranean port.
I have lain awake all night
on the ribs of a luggage rack, smiling at the thought
of hearing his voice again.

The scene unfolds: the village pattering with talk and shopping
    feet,
unmindful of this Homeric return, the stride, unannounced,
    up the hill of my birth.
I practise my greetings on the street,
the old quarrel tucked, with others, in family earth.

But this is where the tape spools out, the door opens to black.
And when I call his name in the house, the house does not
    call back.

Red

I loved my father, the big, loud man
who told stories and laughed.

His young brother, Peter,
hair red as a bed of embers, died in the war.

Reeling down from the hatch of the tank,
he crashed by the radio. Someone the other end
heard his voice: 'I'm killed.'

The dark in my father which cracked out then
was the stuff he drank for the rest of his life.
There was never enough.

One day, sorting papers in his desk, I found in a drawer
embers flaring, strands of fire, a lock of hair.

9/12

The day after the day, dust drifting,
we closed the curtains and went to bed.
A primal imperative, twilit,
amnesiac.

And there he was engendered, insisting on life,
demanding from hopelessness hope,
and in that wavering light, his due
constancy of love.

Home

I forget who told me; seemed surprised I didn't know.
Discreet, red brick: strange I hadn't noticed it
there in plain view from the bridge, on the old meadow.
Someone buzzed me in. 'Private,' I thought, glancing at the walls.
But clean and bright. Fine, as homes for old people go.

The girl in reception smiled. 'So you're here today.'
And though I knew this was a dream, my cheek burned.
'He's frail, as you'd expect, but cheerful in his way.'
'Listen,' I smiled. 'My father's dead, gone twenty years.'
No,' she replied. 'He was here all the time. It's you that went away.'

Allegro con brio

Grass, A Blessing

On all grass, true grasses, sedges, rushes. Lawn grass, clippered
    close like a boy's head,
mozzy drone of mower riding it, summery scent, round
    mounds of cuttings in shade,
stick your arm in an oven-warm pie of it.

Thinning grass of public parks, plush once, patched now like
    a dog's manged back
by illegal barbies, post-weekend, hundreds and thousands'd
    with bottles, hairgrips,
ready as ever to heft the magic carpet of a picnic.

Turf, superior, sporty stuff, spruced for the feet of blazered
    members, pale square
holy-rollered; grass courts grass, sprinkled when needed,
    primped, made up with cool lime lines; a
blessing on you, grass, all species of grass, a kiss, a benison.

Meadow grass, in plots concealed by stumbling walls forgotten
    by farmer, rare and lush as love in
secret, cradling troves of poppy, cow-parsley. And last not
    least, cliff-top grass, on you grateful
benediction, unkempt, tousled with thrift, tough salt crop.

On grass, all grass. Grass to sprawl on, play on, run on, grass
    to eat on, sit and read on,
cry on, love on, lie and look up at clouds or gyring stars on,
    thank you for being
here, persistent, resistant to destruction, and green. So green.

Hullo Bridge, Coverdale

Called so because, centuries past,
we two met, once and again,
at these piled stones spanning the banks;
Hall and Common, prised apart by the copper Cover.
Met and named it for our greeting,
pressed that name to the lips of our children.

Later, maps plucked it from water,
set it for travellers beyond our horizon.

And further on, when maps are mouldered to leaf again,
will the name still engender in friends and lovers
its gentle entreaty to tryst or liaison?
Will you and I, in the skin of others,
strip and lean on the wall of the wind
in the arm of the bridge?

Kirkgate Sequence

Poems commissioned for engraving
on stone benches in Kirkgate, Leeds.

1.

I love you
but nothing is set
in stone.

Hot cinder
the look he threw me
across the lane.

Look after the pennies.
The banks will look after
themselves.

In the narrow street
between God and market
slips the secret.

Be tender with time.
Stroke the skin
of every minute.

Weather writes
the only words
stone remembers.

2.

Drop your bag,
and instead of your own
a tumble of other things
spill on the paving:
compact, clay pipe,
fish knife, pouch of snuff.

Who were we?
Who comes after?
What of ours will they carry?

3.

Shopper, dreamer,
beneath your foot,
two yards deep,
the print of my own
treads lightly, set in clay
as I strolled Kirkgate
to meet my girl
ten lives ago.

4.

Remember weather, change in the breeze,
if worry nags or memory tugs at the sleeve.

When hope is lean and the heart lacks,
try the door to the Theatre de Luxe.

Lift your head, remember the sky,
when worlds are flat and level holds the eye.

If limbs are thick and feet have nowhere to go,
sit for a while by an open window.

When ice melts and continents drift,
give what you own to love and not to thrift.

Here is Something

A creature of light
pullulates gently on the door.
Like a studied virus on a screen,
it pops itself and shuts, then glows again.
A simple thing, the sun through trees
made miracle by frosted glass.

Knee-Pit

Knee-pit: vale unnamed, unodorous;
lost resort which fingers rarely visit
save to scratch.

Armpit, ah, is coy with promise,
sloping to places we wish to go.
The pimple of sweat that slips from shade to nipple –
where does humble knee-pit lead?
To sock and ankle.

Pity knee-pit, stooge to knee,
(the flashy joint that springs and swivels,
then in mid-age grumbles to pain).
Does knee-pit complain? Ever chewed pills
for knee-pit, smoothed on cream?

Plain, unlauded. B-side, dark side of the moon.
Unloved park at the edge of town, unfrequented room.
Friend, I beg, when next the hand or mouth go travelling,
tickle the one who seldom smiles. Coax with tongue
the introvert place that does not plump or glisten for love,
but waits. Go down.
Go further down.

After the Event

Before, my favourite was a pair
of handmade loafers, cushion-soled.

But they weren't the ones I grabbed
the night of the raid.

The shoes I took on the road
were my old walkers, cross-laced.

When they wore through I was pleased to find
some military boots discarded in a stream.

They were taken off me. That's when a dead man
lent me his sandals.

Now, barefoot, my soles are yellowed and tough
though I still avoid glass.

Once, if I felt a rub on the heel,
I would sit on a bench, take off my shoe,

Shake into the grass
a tiny sand-brown pebble.

The Laughing Woman

(a ghost story)

My mother spoke of her often.
Summer nights, the low easy notes
carried on stone-warmed air.

Throw off the sheet, run to the sill.
My mother, at thirty, unwisely married,
looks down into the castle quad from her open window.

And there it is again, like a bird's bebop, a ripple of glass.
A self-possessed laugh.

Look, the tail of a ballroom dress.
Here, in the darkness of an arch, the pale oval
of a face thrown back.

The laughing woman, what is she laughing at?
The vanity of trouble, the necessity of sleep?

As if they are all together, the dead,
in a bar, dancing, laughing their heads off
and this one reveller has just stepped out for a breath,
before, smiling, toss of the hair, she strolls back in.

He Tells the Story Often

I, on the other hand

remember nothing about that night, except the ice cream; oh and Elias rolling his sleeve and plunging his hand into the vat; the ring was his mother's. Leave it, said Rose, it might in any case have gone between the boards. Or in Phil's pocket. A man who nobody knew sat in the corner ripping pages from The Golden Notebook as David was sick in the house fern.

I, on the other hand

stone blood sober, leant on the cooker, fag in the brim of my crumpled Stetson. Thank the Lord I found my harmonica before Jan remembered she had her violin. Foggy Foggy Dew, I think I played, as Jack fell asleep on the round table, his hand still cupping the Spanish girl's breast. She was very far gone, and later left in a cab with Matt.

I, on the other hand

woke with the central heating in Farzana's flat, sun in my face, my feet on a dog. He didn't seem to mind and always, apparently, slept with Farzana. Fazz herself, who I'd spoken to once near the vending machine, was out in the kitchen, singing a kettle to the boil. 'Shout, shout, let it all out.' When she came in later with jasmine tea, she was not completely naked.

I, on the other hand –

To the Absence

I have been here before
with coffee at a window table
waiting for your face
to fill an oval of air.

I had scoped today
around our meeting,
plans accreting to noon
and the sighting of you.
But the snow, of course.

It could be worse.
Once my life wagged
on the due north of your promise.
This time, just in case,
I brought a book.
It's a good one.

Keeping On

You forget how rivers keep on.
Way south, on the A1, a sign tells me
I've crossed the Swale.

Is that the Swale that gargles rocks,
sashaying down through East Gill Force,
Wain Wath?

Of course. The Swale won't stop,
just because the drama is done
and we've stopped watching.

Like spotting an actor or singer in the paper.
'Is he still playing, still keeping on?'

Perhaps the deepest and fullest is to come.
Lower land, a statelier bend. A dreamier purling
beneath that bridge in the market town.

And still the Ure to join
in a plaiding of temperatures, colours, currents.
The sea to find.

Reveille: Lawnswood Cemetery

You, late sleepers, lier-inners,
dreamers in dormitories of slate and marble.
Look what you miss by dozing on!

The sky is awake, the morning
metal with frost, it shines. And will fade. Rise,
wasters, lie-a-bedders. Hands off cocks.
Dig your pointy elbows in,
look sharp.

Like Spencer's children,
toss stone-blanket, splash skin with sun,
comb from hair the rags of earth.
Be quick.